cat names

cat names

Jenny Linford

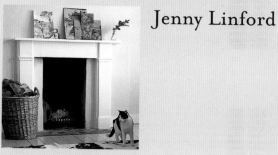

RYLAND
PETERS
& SMALL

LONDON NEW YORK

Designer Iona Hoyle
Senior Editor Miriam Hyslop
Picture Researcher Emily Westlake
Production Gordana Simakovic
Art Director Anne-Marie Bulat
Publishing Director Alison Starling

First published in the United States in 2006
by Ryland Peters & Small, Inc.
519 Broadway, 5th Floor
New York, NY 10012
www.rylandpeters.com

10 9 8 7 6 5 4 3 2 1

Text, design, and photography
© Ryland Peters & Small 2006

ISBN-10: 1-84597-274-0
ISBN-13: 978-1-84597-274-5

Printed and bound in China

contents

introduction

Bringing home a tiny kitten is one of life's great pleasures. Owning a new kitten, however, does bring with it a particular dilemma. What should this lovely little creature be called? It's so important to find a name that you really like and that suits your new feline companion. While, of course, fundamental names like Cat or Puss continue to be popular, there is a rich seam of possible cat names to mine. Choose from names that reflect your cat's coloring, like Java or Ebony, or ones that refer to its personality, so Napoleon for small, fighting tom-cats or Artemis for predatory females. Name your cat after famous literary or historic felines such as President Clinton's White House cat, Socks, Humphrey the Downing Street cat, or T.S. Eliot's mystery cat, Macavity. With over a thousand names to choose from, naming your new cat has never been so easy or so much fun.

classic cats

Aladdin
For adventurous tomcats.

Allegro
A musical name for lively cats.

Alley cat
For felines of either sex.

Amaretto
For cats of either sex, after
the sweet Italian almond-
flavored liqueur.

Ari
From the Hebrew for "lion."

Aristocat
For noble, aristocratic felines
of either sex.

Banshee
For vocal cats prone to wailing.

Beethoven
A musical name for male
cats, after the great German
composer.

Bibi
For attractive female cats,
from the French *beaublot*,
meaning "trinket."

Bingo
For lucky cats, after the game.

Bistro
For greedy cats of either sex,
after the French eaterie.

Blackie
A no-nonsense name for
black cats of either sex.

Blade
For dashing tomcats.

Bobcat
For tough tomcats, after the
short-tailed wild cat.

Bongo
A music-inspired name for
rhythmic cats.

Bonsai
For diminutive cats of either sex,
after the miniature trees.

Boots
For cats whose markings feature
elegant white "boots."

Bourbon
For mellow cats of either sex,
inspired by the smooth
Southern whiskey.

Bowie
For vocal, charismatic cats, after
rock star David Bowie.

Brains
The perfect name for super-
intelligent cats.

Bramble
For sharp-clawed cats.

Brat
For cats good at getting their
own way.

Bubbles
A humorous name, suitable for
air-headed felines of either sex.

Buttons
For bright-eyed cats.

Cactus
A plant-inspired name for cats with prickly claws.

Calypso
A music-inspired name for rhythmic cats.

Candy
An appropriate name for sweet-natured cats of either sex.

Cashmere
For soft, fluffy cats of either sex.

Cat
A fundamental but much-loved name, given to many felines.

Charleston
For rhythmic cats after the classic dance.

Chat
A classic cat name (pronounced "sha"), from the French for "cat."

Cheeky
For cats who always want more.

Cheetah
For fleet-footed cats of either sex.

Chéri
For beloved cats, from the French for "dear." Chérie is the female version.

Cherry
A fruit-inspired name.

China
For cats of either sex.

Chives
An herb-inspired name for cats of either sex.

Christmas
A festive name for cats of either sex, especially appropriate for those brought home over the holiday season.

Chutney
A food-inspired name for cats of either sex.

Claws
For spiky cats of either sex.

Crackers
A humorous name for cats of either sex.

Crumpet
A homey name for domestic cats.

Crystal
For bright-eyed cats, from the Greek for "ice."

Cuddles
For affectionate cats of either sex.

Curious
For nosy cats of either sex.

Cuzco
A Latin American name for cats of either sex.

Dash
For lively, run-around cats.

Data
A *Star Trek: The Next Generation*-inspired name for intelligent technocats.

Diamond
For bright-eyed cats.

Diesel
For cats with loud, throaty purrs.

Dill
An herb-inspired name for cats of either sex.

Dixie
A jazz-inspired name for cats of either sex.

Dumpling
For plump cats of either sex.

Egypt
For Sphinx-like cats of either sex.

Elba
For solitary cats of either sex, after the Italian island to which Napoleon was exiled.

ET
For unearthly cats, inspired by Spielberg's extraterrestrial creation.

Fang
For toothy cats of either sex.

Fat Cat
For chubby cats of either sex.

Fats
For portly tomcats, after jazz musician Fats Domino.

Fatty
For plump cats of either sex.

Felice
An Italian name for good-natured cats, from the Italian for "happy."

Fig
A fruit-inspired name for cats of either sex.

Flipflop
For relaxed, lazy felines of either sex.

Fluff
For long-haired cats.

Frisky
For energetic, playful cats of either sex.

Furball
An affectionate name for cats of either sex.

Furry
A self-explanatory name for cats of either sex.

Gadget
For inventive cats of either sex.

Ganesha
For portly cats, after the elephant-headed Hindu god.

Garlic
A culinary name for cats of either sex.

Gato
For cats of either sex, from the Spanish for "cat."

Gemini
An astrological name for cats, especially those with a dual nature.

Gizmo
For inventive cats of either sex. Also for gremlin-like felines.

Griffin
For leonine cats of either sex, after the mythical creature with a lion's body and the head and wings of an eagle.

Grimalkin
A traditional cat's name, especially used for black cats, often associated with witchcraft and magic.

Hairball
An affectionate name for long-furred cats.

Harrison
After Harrison Weir, a famous cat breeder.

Heinz
A classic cat's name, with Heinz noted for its 57 varieties.

Hero
A noble name, suitable for cats of either sex.

Hiss
An expressive sibilant name for bad-tempered cats.

Holly
The perfect name for sharp-clawed Christmas kittens.

Hong Kong
A cosmopolitan name for food-loving cats, with Hong Kong noted for its excellent Chinese cuisine.

Hunter
A self-explanatory name for killer cats.

Jazz
A music-inspired name for cats of either sex.

Jelly
For sweet-natured felines of either sex.

Jewel
For precious cats of either sex.

Juniper
A plant-inspired name for cats of either sex.

Ketchup
A food-inspired name for greedy cats.

Killer
A classic name for predatory hunter cats.

King
For regal male cats.

Kitty
A classic feline name.

Koh-I-Noor
A jewel-inspired name for bright-eyed cats, after the famous diamond.

Krazy Kat
For mad felines, after the cult comic strip cat.

Kumquat
A fruit-inspired name for cats of either sex, after the small tangy citrus fruit.

Leica
For sharp-eyed cats of either sex, after the prestigious camera, noted for its lens quality.

Lentil
A food-inspired name for cats of either sex.

Lettuce
A salad-inspired name for garden-loving cats.

Libra
A zodiac-inspired name for well-balanced cats.

Lilliput
For small cats of either sex, after the miniature land in *Gulliver's Travels*.

Lobster
For cats with a fondness for seafood.

London
A capital British name for city-dwelling tomcats.

Lotus
A flower-inspired name for serene female cats, especially suitable for beautiful cats.

Lucky
An appropriate name for lucky black cats of either sex.

Luna
For night-loving cats, from the Italian for "moon."

Macaroni
A food-inspired name for cats of either sex.

Malt
An old-fashioned name for cats of either sex.

Matty
A down-to-earth name.

Mau
An appealingly phonetic name, from the Egyptian for "cat."

Maverick
For independent-minded cats.

Maze
For cats who tend to get lo[st]

Meep
An expressive monosyllabic name for cats of either sex.

Melissa
For sweet-natured female cats, from the Greek for "bee."

Melody
A music-inspired name for female cats.

Meow
For vocal cats of either sex.

Midge
For small, lively cats of either sex.

Minou
The French equivalent to "Kitty."

Mog
A down-to-earth name for cats of either sex, also used as a term for alley cats.

Moon
A lunar name for night-loving cats of either sex.

Mouser
For feline hunters of either sex.

Muesli
A food-inspired name for healthy cats of either sex.

Muffin
A food-inspired name for sweet-natured cats.

Noodles
A food-inspired name for greedy cats.

Oats
A food-inspired name for healthy cats of either sex.

Opal
A gemstone-inspired name for bright-eyed cats of either sex.

Padfoot
For soft-pawed cats of either sex.

Papyrus
An Egyptian name for slender cats of either sex, after the reed-like plant.

Patch
A much-loved name for patchwork cats of either sex.

Peach
A fruit-inspired name for soft-furred cats.

Pesto
A food-inspired name for cats of either sex.

Piccolo
For small male cats, from the Italian for "little." Piccola is the female version.

Pickles
A food-inspired name for cats of either sex.

Pilchard
A food-inspired name for fish-loving felines of either sex.

Pizza
A food-inspired name for speedy cats, after the popular fast food.

Polka
A dance-inspired name for lively cats of either sex.

Pomegranate
A fruit-inspired name for sweet-natured cats.

Pookie
A classic cat name.

Popcorn
A snack-inspired name for lively cats of either sex.

Poppy
A flower-inspired name for pretty female felines.

Puck
For swift-footed, mischievous cats, after Shakespeare's fairy messenger in *A Midsummer Night's Dream*.

Pudding
An affectionate, humorous name for fat cats.

Purrball
An affectionate name for purry cats of either sex.

Purry
A classic name for friendly cats.

Puss
The classic name for either male or female felines.

Puss-in-Boots
For clever tomcats, from the traditional fairytale.

Pussy
A popular name for female felines.

Ra
For sun-loving cats, after the Egyptian sun god.

Rascal
For cheeky cats who are apt to get up to mischief.

Raspberry
A fruit-inspired name for cats of either sex.

Ratatouille
A food-inspired name, after the Mediterranean dish.

River
An aquatic-inspired name for cats that love to play with water.

Rocket
For energetic, fast-moving cats of either sex.

Rollmop
A humorous name for fish-loving cats, after the pickled herring dish.

Roma
For cosmopolitan cats, after the Italian capital city.

Sago
A homey food-inspired name for cats of either sex.

Salmon
For fish-loving cats of either sex.

Savoy
For elegant cats, after London's world-famous hotel.

Scat
For vocal cats, after the jazz style of singing.

Scrabble
For intelligent cats of either sex, after the popular word game.

Scratchy
For sharp-clawed cats.

Sesame
A seed-inspired name for male or female cats.

Shandy
A drink-inspired name for cats of either sex.

Shrimp
For small cats of either sex.

Sicily
For sun-loving cats of either sex, after the Italian island.

Sioux
For hunting cats, after the Native American tribe.

Sky
For outdoor-loving felines of either sex.

Snagglepuss
For sharp-clawed felines of either sex.

Soy
For healthy male cats.

Spice
An aromatic name for male or female cats.

Strawberry
A fruit-inspired name for sweet-natured cats of either sex.

Succotash
A vegetable-inspired name for cats of either sex.

Sudoku
A puzzle-inspired name for thoughtful cats.

Summer
A season-inspired name for sun-loving cats of either sex.

Sushi
For fish-loving felines, after the traditional Japanese dish.

Sweetie
An affectionate name for cats of either sex.

Symi
A sibilant name for cats of either sex.

Taco
A food-inspired name for greedy cats.

Talisman
For lucky cats of either sex.

Tamarind
A food-inspired name for cats of either sex.

Tango
A dance-inspired name for seductive felines.

Tartan
A Scottish-inspired name for cats of either sex.

Tequila
A Mexican-inspired name for spirited females, after the potent alcoholic drink.

Thistle
For sharp-clawed cats of either sex.

Thyme
An herb-inspired name for cats of either sex.

Tibbles
An affectionate name for cats of either sex.

Tiddles
A popular name for cats of either sex.

Tiffin
For greedy cats, after the Indian name for a light lunch.

Tokyo
For city-dwelling cats, after the capital city of Japan.

Tomato
A food-inspired name for cats of either sex.

Tonka
A spice-inspired name for cats of either sex, after the tonka bean.

Trombone
A music-inspired name for vocal cats of either sex.

Truffle
A food-inspired name for greedy cats of either sex.

Tucker
A jolly name for food-loving cats.

Tufty
A humorous name for spiky-haired cats.

Vanilla
A spice-inspired name for female felines.

Velvet
For soft-furred cats of either sex.

Venice
For water-loving cats, after the Italian city built on over a hundred islands.

Vodka
A spirit-inspired name for cats of either sex.

Waffles
A food-inspired name for cats of either sex.

Whiskers
A classic name for cats of either sex.

Wildcat
For wild cats of either sex.

Willow
For cats of either sex who like climbing trees.

Wobble
An affectionate name for cats of either sex.

Wonton
For plump cats, after the popular bite-sized Chinese dumpling.

Yoga
For flexible, mellow cats.

Yoyo
For frenetic cats of either sex.

Yum Yum
For greedy cats of either sex.

Zanzibar
A tropical name for cats of either sex.

Zucchero
For sweet-natured cats, from the Italian for "sugar."

pedigree cats

Abyssinia
A majestic name for cats of either sex, especially good for Abyssinian cats.

Amber
For yellow- or orange-eyed female felines.

Angora
A classic name for soft-furred cats such as Angoras.

Aqua
For water-loving cats such as Turkish Vans, from the Italian for "water."

Astrakhan
For curly-coated cats of either sex, after the distinctive fabric.

Bamboo
For cats of either sex of Eastern origins such as Siamese, after the graceful tropical giant grass.

Blue
A classic name, ideal for smoky-blue pedigree cats.

Buddha
A name for serene cats, especially suitable for Oriental cats.

Bunny
An affectionate name for Manx cats, with their "bunny-hop" gait.

Burma
Classic name for Burmese cats.

Captain Jenks
For Maine Coons, after the "first" Maine cat, shown at New York cat shows in 1861.

Champagne
For sparkling pedigree cats, after the famous French wine.

Chatty
For talkative Siamese cats of either sex.

Chiang Mai
For Siamese cats of either sex, after the town in northwest Thailand famous for its picturesque temples.

Copper
After the reddish-brown metal, especially suitable for Red Abyssinians.

Cuba
A geographical name for Havana Browns.

Curly
For long-haired curly cats, such as La Perm and Selkirk Rex.

Cymru
For Cymric or Long-haired Manxes, from the Welsh name for "Wales."

Dolly
An affectionate name for female Ragdolls.

Feng Shui
For calm cats.

Gamelan
For Balinese cats, after the percussive Indonesian orchestra.

Geisha
For Oriental female cats.

Gingko
A tree-inspired name for Oriental cats of either sex.

Ginseng
For cats of either sex, after the root used in Chinese medicine.

Gold
For golden-eyed cats, such as Maine Coons.

Happy
A cheerful name for Ragdoll cats noted for their sweet nature and docile temperaments.

Indonesia
A geographical name for Balinese cats.

Istanbul
For Turkish Angoras, after the historic Turkish city.

Jade
For prized cats of either sex, after the semi-precious stone.

Jump
For athletic, leaping cats, such as Cornish Rexes.

Kallibunker
For Cornish Rexes, after the original Cornish Rex born in 1950.

Karate
For fast-moving, combative Oriental cats, after the martial arts form that originated in Japan.

Kiku
For pretty female Oriental cats, from the Japanese for "chrysanthemum."

Kirlee
After the curly-coated cat who founded the Devon Rex breed.

Ko Samui
For pretty Siamese cats, after the lovely Thai island, which is also a popular tourist destination.

Lamb
An endearing name for gentle curly-haired cats of either sex, such as Cornish or Devon Rexes.

Lilac
A flower-inspired name for gray-furred female felines—especially apt for Russian Blues, as "lilac" is the term given to warm-toned gray fur.

Litchee
A fruit-inspired name for Burmese and Siamese cats of either sex.

Mandalay
For Burmese cats, after the famous Burmese town.

Maneki-neko
For Japanese bobtails, immortalized in Japan as the famous beckoning cat, a good luck symbol.

Manx
A classic name for tail-less or Manx cats, rumored to be descended from cats on the ships of the Spanish Armada.

Misty
For silver-coated Nebelung cats.

Mousehole
For Cornish Rexes, after the English fishing village famous for its "Mousehole cat."

Mulberry
For Persian cats, inspired by the mulberry, a popular Persian fruit.

Munchkin
A classic name for short-legged Munchkin cats.

Myanmar
For Burmese and Birman cats, after the Burmese capital.

Norway
For Norwegian Forest cats.

Omar
A poetic name for Persian tomcats, after the Persian poet Omar Khayyam, famous for his "Rubaiyat."

Orchid
A flower-inspired name for beautiful Siamese cats.

Oslo
For Norwegian Forest cats, after the capital of Norway.

Peony
A flower-inspired name, suitable for female Oriental cats.

Persia
A classic name for Persian cats.

Pest
The first Selkirk Rex, shortened from Miss DePesto of NoFace.

Pixie
For American Curl cats.

Platinum
For silver cats, after the rare, costly metal.

Plymouth
For Devon Rexes, after the port in the south of England.

Poodle
For curly-coated cats, such as Rexes.

Rabbit
For Ruddy Abyssinian cats, also known as the "rabbit cat."

Rangoon
For Burmese cats, after the former name of the capital of Burma.

Rex
From the Latin for "king," a name for regal male cats, especially suitable for Rex cats.

Rosso
For red-coated cats, from the Italian for "red."

Russia
A classic name for Russian Blues.

Saffron
For costly cats of either sex, inspired by the most expensive spice in the world.

St. Ives
For Cornish Rexes, after the seaside town in England.

Shulamith
The name of the first American Curl cat, from which all Curls trace their origins.

Siam
For Siamese cats, after the ancient name for Thailand.

Silk
For pedigree cats with silky soft fur.

Sinatra
For vocal blue-eyed tomcats, after singer Frank Sinatra, known as "Ol' Blue Eyes."

Singapore
A classic name for Singapura cats of either sex.

Si-Sawat
For Eastern cats, after the description of a cat from Korat given in Thailand's historic *Cat-Book Poems*.

Snooks
The name of an early Scottish Fold cat.

Snow
For thick-furred cats, such as Maine Coons.

Somali
For Abyssinian and Somali cats.

Spotty
A humorous name for Ocicat cats of either sex, known for their spotted coats.

pedigree cats

21

Stargazy
For Cornish Rexes, after the
famous Cornish fish pie.

Tang
An ancient Chinese name,
especially suitable for Oriental cats.

Tao
A philosophical name for
contemplative cats of either sex,
especially Oriental ones.

Tiffanie
An elegant name for silky-soft
Tiffanie cats.

Tokyo
For Japanese Bobtails, after the
Japanese capital.

Tolstoy
A Russian literary name for
impressive Siberian Forest cats.

Tonga
For Ocicats, after one of the
breed's founding cats.

Tortie
A classic name for tortoiseshell
felines of either sex.

Turquoise
A stone-inspired name for blue-
eyed pedigrees of either sex.

Ubud
For Balinese cats, after the
historic town on the island of Bali.

Wegie
A diminutive name for
Norwegian Forest cats.

Wong Mau
The founder of the American
Burmese breed.

Yeti
For long-haired cats, after
the Abominable Snowman.

Yul
For regal Siamese tomcats—
after Yul Brynner, the actor
who played the King of Siam
in *The King and I.*

Zen
A Buddhist-inspired name
for serene cats of either sex,
especially Oriental ones.

Zenobia
For formidable, regal female
cats, after the warrior queen
of Palmyra, noted for her
military conquests.

Zula
For Abyssinian cats, after one of
the founding cats.

famous felines

Arlene
Garfield's girlfriend.

Bagpuss
The much-loved, magical stripy cat of the classic British children's TV series *Bagpuss*.

Caruso
The operatic name given to nineteenth-century writer Edward Gosse's stately cat.

Cheshire Cat
For good-natured male cats, after the cat with a huge grin created by Lewis Carroll in *Alice in Wonderland*.

Clarence
After gentle cross-eyed lion in the popular 1960s TV series *Daktari*.

D.C.
Siamese crime-solving cat in Disney's *That Darn Cat*.

Deuteronomy
A venerable name after T.S. Eliot's long-lived feline in *Old Possum's Book of Practical Cats*.

Dinah
Alice in Wonderland's cat in Lewis Carroll's classic tale.

Duchess
The elegant white feline star of Disney's *The Aristocats*.

Figaro
Geppetto's furry friend in the Disney adaptation of *Pinocchio*.

Franchette
The elegant name given to Claudine's beloved cat in Colette's novel *Claudine at School*.

Garfield
The ultimate cartoon slob cat, devoted to lasagne and leading a life of leisure.

Griddlebone
From T.S. Eliot's *Old Possum's Book of Practical Cats*, the name given to Growltiger's faithless feline companion.

Growltiger
T.S. Eliot's rough "Bravo Cat," from *Old Possum's Book of Practical Cats*.

Gus
T.S. Eliot's "theater cat" from *Old Possum's Book of Practical Cats*.

Heathcliff
The mischievous cartoon cat.

Hinca
The name of Scottish author Sir Walter Scott's "favorite cat," a notable hunter and fighter.

Hodge
The name of Dr. Johnson's "very fine cat," for whom, according to Boswell, "he himself used to go out and buy oysters."

Humphrey
A political name for suave tomcats. After Humphrey the cat who lives at No. 10 Downing Street, the home of Britain's serving Prime Minister.

Jellicle
Fun-loving, black and white cats, from T.S. Eliot's *Old Possum's Book of Practical Cats*.

Jennie
The feline heroine of Paul Gallico's novel *Jennie*, about a boy turned into a cat who is lovingly protected by Jennie.

Jennyanydots
T.S. Eliot's "gumbie cat" with "tiger stripes and leopard spots," from *Old Possum's Book of Practical Cats*.

Jeffrey
The name of the eighteenth-century poet Christopher Smart's cat, immortalized in Smart's wonderful piece of poetry "My Cat Jeffrey;" especially appropriate for striped cats, as Jeffrey "is of the tribe of Tiger."

Korky the Cat
A famous, saucy cartoon cat, featured in the British comic *Dandy*.

Lillian
An affectionate cat with a taste for liqueur, portrayed by Damon Runyon in an eponymous short story.

Macavity
T.S. Eliot's "mystery cat," from *Old Possum's Book of Practical Cats*, a stealthy ginger cat known as "The Hidden Paw."

Major
The name given to poet Stevie Smith's cat, about whom she wrote, "Major is a fine cat."

The Master's Cat
The name given by Charles Dickens's servants to the household cat who adored the Victorian novelist and followed him about like a dog.

Mehitabel
The elegant feline star of Don Marquis's quirky books about Archie the New York cockroach and his friend Mehitabel the cat.

Ming
An elegant name with Eastern associations from Patricia Highsmith's story "Ming's Biggest Prey."

Minnaloushe
The name given to a black cat by the poet W.B. Yeats in his poem "The Cat and the Moon."

Mistoffelees
The clever, small black tomcat from T.S. Eliot's *Old Possum's Book of Practical Cats*.

Mouschi
The endearing name given to Anne Frank's cat, who kept her company while she was in hiding from the Nazis.

Mr. Bigglesworth
Dr. Evil's pet in *Austin Powers*.

Mrs. Norris
The bad-tempered Hogwarts School cat from J.K. Rowling's Harry Potter books.

Mungojerrie
T.S. Eliot's crime-loving cat, from *Old Possum's Book of Practical Cats*.

Nelson
The patriotic and heroic name given to Winston Churchill's wartime headquarters cat during World War II.

O'Malley
The handsome alley cat from Disney's *The Aristocats*.

Pluto
The name given to the clever cat in Edgar Allan Poe's macabre story "The Black Cat."

Rum Tum
T.S. Eliot's perverse cat, immortalized in *Old Possum's Book of Practical Cats*.

Rumpelteazer
T.S. Eliot's cat burglar from *Old Possum's Book of Practical Cats*.

Rumpuscat
A great, fearsome feline who gives battle in T.S. Eliot's *Old Possum's Book of Practical Cats*.

Saha
The elegant feline portrayed by Colette in a compelling eponymous short story.

Scratchy
The "cartoon" cat from *The Simpsons*—always trying (and failing) to get the better of Itchy the Mouse. For cats that fancy themselves as a bit of a hunter.

Selima
The dainty cat in Thomas Gray's poem "Ode on the Death of a Favourite Cat, Drowned in a Tub of Gold Fishes."

Shere Khan
The ferocious tiger in Kipling's *Jungle Book*.

Simon
A heroic black and white tomcat whose World War II naval career earned him the animal VC.

Si
One of the mischievous cats in Disney's *Lady and the Tramp*.

Sir John Langborn
The distinguished name given to the English writer Jeremy Bentham's cat.

Skimbleshanks
T.S. Eliot's green-eyed "railway cat" from *Old Possum's Book of Practical Cats*.

Slippers
The affectionate name given to Mrs. Theodore Roosevelt's gray, six-toed White House cat.

Snowdrop
The dainty name given to Alice's white kitten in *Alice Through the Looking Glass*.

Socks
President Clinton's White House cat.

Sylvester
The foolish black-and-white cartoon cat, forever chasing Tweety Pie.

Tammany
One of Mark Twain's cats, whom he called "the most beautiful cat on the western bulge of the globe."

Tobermory
The wickedly observant cat in Saki's witty tale of a cat with the gift of speech.

Tom Kitten
The name of Beatrix Potter's famous fictional naughty kitten.

Tom Quartz
The name given by President Theodore Roosevelt to his "cunningest kitten."

Top Cat
The quick-witted alley cat, star of an eponymous TV cartoon series.

Tortoise
The name of a tortoiseshell tabby in George Elliot's novel *Middlemarch*.

Webster
The large, black composed cat who featured in P.G. Wodehouse's "Story of Webster."

Willie
President George W. Bush's cat.

girl cats

Alice
For female cats who like exploring, after Lewis Carroll's *Alice in Wonderland*.

Amazing Grace
For vocal females.

Amélie
A French name for pretty females.

Amourette
A dainty name which means "beloved" in French.

Andromeda
For noble females, after the princess of Greek mythology.

Angel Cake
For delicious felines.

Angel Face
For beautiful felines.

Aria
An operatic name for vocal female felines.

Artemis
For nocturnal huntresses, after the goddess of the moon.

Atalanta
For swift-footed female felines, after the famous huntress of Greek mythology.

Audrey
For elegant females, after the gamine actress Audrey Hepburn.

Ava
A glamorous female name, after film star Ava Gardner.

Babe
For appealing felines.

Babs
Endearing feminine diminutive of Barbara.

Bam Bam
For characterful females.

Bella
A melodic name for lovely female felines, from the Italian for "beautiful."

Belladonna
Especially appropriate for female black cats, after the plant associated with witches.

Belle
An elegant name for attractive female felines, from the French for "beautiful."

Billie
A jazz-inspired name for vocal felines, after the great jazz singer Billie Holiday.

Birdie
For birdwatching felines who are fascinated by their feathered friends.

Boadicea
For combative queenly females, after the courageous Queen of the Iceni who rebelled against the Romans.

Calliope
For vocal female felines, after the Greek muse of eloquence.

Cara
An affectionate name for beloved female cats, after the Italian for "dear."

Carmen
An operatic name for dramatic, beautiful female cats, after the heroine of Bizet's opera.

Cassandra
A legendary name for characterful female cats, after the Trojan princess.

Catherine
For imperial felines, after the eighteenth-century Empress of Russia.

Chantilly
For dainty females, after the famous French lace.

Chrysanthemum
A floral name for female felines.

Cleopatra
For captivating female felines, after the beautiful Queen of Egypt.

Coco
For elegant cats, after French fashion designer Coco Chanel.

Colette
For elegant female cats, after the French author Colette, who adored cats and frequently wrote about them.

Daisy
A floral name, inspired by the white and yellow flower, for small, pretty female cats.

Daphne
For tree-loving female felines, after the nymph in Greek mythology who was turned into a laurel tree.

Delphi
For perceptive female felines, after the oracle of Delphi in ancient Greece.

Demeter
For fruitful female felines, after the Greek goddess of harvest, mother of Persephone.

Diana
For female felines who excel at nocturnal hunting, after the Roman goddess of the hunt, associated with the moon.

Doris
For wholesome female cats, inspired by film star Doris Day, who portrayed the archetypal "girl next door."

Dot
An affectionate, monosyllabic name.

Eartha
For attractive female felines, after husky-voiced singer Eartha Kitt, who starred as a sexy Catwoman in 1960s cult TV series *Batman*.

Elizabeth
A regal cat name, after British queens Elizabeth I and II.

Ella
For musical female felines, after the American chanteuse Ella Fitzgerald.

Emma
For strong-willed female felines, after the heroine of Jane Austen's eponymous novel.

Fifi
A dainty name with a French flavor.

Fiji
A tropical name for cats of either sex, inspired by the Pacific island.

Flamenco
For graceful cats of either sex, inspired by the famous Spanish dance.

Flora
For flower-loving female cats, after the Roman goddess of blossoming plants.

Florida
For sun-loving female felines, after the southern state famous for its beach resorts.

Fuchsia
A floral name for beautiful felines, after the scarlet flowering shrub.

Galadriel
For graceful cats, after the beautiful elf in Tolkien's *The Lord of the Rings*.

Garbo
For beautiful, solitary female felines, after the silent film star Greta Garbo.

Girl
A classic name for female felines.

Goa
For beautiful female cats, after the Indian state famed for its palm-fringed beaches.

Grace
For graceful female felines.

Guava
A fruit-inspired name, after the tropical fruit.

Hecuba
For regal female cats, after the mythological Queen of Troy.

Helen
For beautiful female felines, after the lovely Helen of ancient Greek legend.

Hermione
For clever females, after J.K. Rowling's literary heroine Hermione Granger.

Honey
An endearing name for sweet-natured female cats.

Hyacinth
A flower-inspired name for pretty female cats.

India
For beautiful felines, especially suitable for Oriental cat breeds.

Iris
For beautiful female cats, after the Greek mythological messenger of the gods.

Isadora
For graceful female cats, after dancer Isadora Duncan.

Isis
For awe-inspiring female cats, after the powerful ancient Egyptian goddess, devoted mother of Horus.

Isolde
Wagnerian name for operatic cats.

Ivy
A plant-inspired name for female cats of a clinging nature.

Jackie
For graceful felines, inspired by Jackie Kennedy, noted for her elegance.

Jemima
For docile cats, from the Arab *jomima* meaning "dove."

Jessie
A pretty name for female felines.

Jezebel
A biblical name for tempestuous female felines.

Juno
For queenly female cats; in Roman mythology, Juno was the wife of Jupiter.

Kelly
A Hollywood name for elegant felines, after cool, blonde actress Grace Kelly.

Lavender
A floral name for fragrant female cats.

Leia
A *Star Wars*-inspired name for brave, regal females, after Princess Leia.

Lillie
For captivating female cats, with a theatrical stake, after the charming Edwardian actress Lillie Langtry.

Liza
A musical name for large-eyed vocal female felines, inspired by singer Liza Minnelli.

Louise
A cinema-inspired name for sleek elegant female felines, inspired by beautiful 1920s film star Louise Brooks.

Mabel
An old-fashioned name for female felines.

Madeira
For sweet-natured female cats, after the dessert wine and cake.

Madeline
For dainty females.

Madonna
A pop-inspired name for charismatic female felines.

Mae
For voluptuous, seductive female felines, after 1930s sex symbol Mae West.

Maggie
A name for strong-willed female felines.

Mamma Cass
An affectionate name for maternal female felines.

Marilyn
A Hollywood name for beautiful female cats, after legendary blonde film star Marilyn Monroe.

Marlene
For large-eyed, elegant female felines, after glamorous film star Marlene Dietrich.

Martha
A homey name for female felines.

Mata Hari
For seductive females, after the Dutch courtesan and dancer.

Medea
For strong-willed female cats, after the princess in Greek mythology who helped Jason steal the Golden Fleece.

Melba
An operatic name for vocal female felines, after Australian soprano Dame Nellie Melba.

Mignon
For dainty female felines, from the French for "dainty."

Mimi
A diminutive name for feminine felines.

Mimosa
A flower-inspired name for graceful felines.

Missy
An affectionate name for female felines.

Naomi
For lithe slim felines, inspired by supermodel Naomi Campbell.

Nastassja
For beautiful felines, after actress Nastassja Kinski, who starred in the film *Cat People*.

Nefertiti
For elegant female felines, after the ancient Egyptian princess.

Olga
A Russian name for felines.

Olive
A Mediterranean name for female felines.

Pandora
A name from Greek mythology for inquisitive female felines.

Paprika
A spice-inspired name for female felines.

Parma
A food-inspired name for greedy female cats, after Italian Parma ham.

Pavlova
For graceful female felines, inspired by the famous Russian ballet dancer Anna Pavlova.

Persephone
For beautiful females, after the daughter of Demeter in Greek mythology.

Piaf
For petite, strong-willed, vocal female cats, after the diminutive French cabaret singer Edith Piaf.

Pompadour
For elegant females, after Madame de Pompadour, mistress of Louis XIV.

Poppy
A flower-inspired name for pretty cats.

Popsie
An affectionate name for felines.

Primrose
A nature-inspired name for dainty female cats, after the delicate yellow wild flower.

Princess
For beautiful, demanding females.

Queenie
An affectionate name for regal cats.

Rita
A Hollywood name for beautiful female felines, after glamorous film star Rita Hayworth.

Ruby
A gem-inspired name for precious female cats.

Sabrina
For elegant cats.

Samantha
For pretty, feminine cats.

Scala
An operatic name for vocal females, after the famous Milan opera house.

Scarlett
For beautiful but demanding females, after Scarlett O'Hara, heroine of *Gone with the Wind*.

Scheherazade
For beguiling females, after the story-teller of the *Thousand and One Nights*.

Sekhmet
For imposing females, after the Egyptian cat goddesses.

Seraphina
For angelic cats, after seraphim, the first order of angels.

She
For dominating females, after Rider Haggard's queen in *She Who Must Be Obeyed*.

Sheba
For queenly felines, inspired by the Queen of Sheba.

Sibyl
For wise female cats; in Greek and Roman mythology the sibyls were divinely inspired prophets.

Sophia
For beautiful, large-eyed female felines, after voluptuous Italian actress Sophia Loren.

Sphinx
For enigmatic females, after the mysterious creature of Greek mythology.

Sugar
For sweet-natured felines.

Sukie
An old-fashioned feminine name.

Sumatra
For female cats, after the Indonesian island.

Sunbeam
For bright, happy felines.

Susie
A traditional female name.

Tahiti
For graceful female cats, after the beautiful Polynesian island.

Tallulah
For elegant females, after glamourous film star Tallulah Bankhead.

Tiffany
A glamorous name for bright-eyed female cats, after the prestigious New York jewelry store noted for its gems.

Tina
A pop-inspired name for energetic, vocal females, after singer Tina Turner.

Tinkerbell
For pretty, light-footed felines after the fairy who joins Peter Pan on his magical adventures.

Tippi
A Hollywood name for cool female felines, after blonde actress Tippi Hedren.

Tobago
For sun-loving cats; after the Caribbean island.

Tootsie
A humorous name for felines.

Twitchet
A dainty name for cats with sensitive whiskers.

Uhura
A *Star Trek*-inspired name for elegant felines, after the glamorous communications officer Lieutenant Uhura.

Venus
For loving, beautiful female felines, after the Roman goddess of love.

Victoria
For queenly female felines, after Queen Victoria, who ruled over the United Kingdom from 1837 to 1901.

Violet
A floral name for pretty cats.

Virago
For strong-willed female felines.

Vivien
A Hollywood name for glamorous green-eyed female felines, after actress Vivien Leigh.

Zia
A pretty name for splendid cats.

Zoe
For elegant felines.

Zsa Zsa
For glamorous felines, after actress Zsa Zsa Gabor.

Zuleika
From the Arabic for "pretty girl."

tomcats

mythology's Adonis beloved by
Aphrodite for his good looks.

Ajax
A good name for large tough
toms, inspired by the hero of
Homer's *Iliad*.

Alexander
For all-conquering male cats,
after the warlike Alexander
the Great.

Alfred
A traditional name for tomcats.

Ali
A snappy name for handsome,
tough toms, after champion
boxer Muhammad Ali.

Ambrose
An old-fashioned name for
tomcats.

Angus
A fine upstanding Scots name,
from Gaelic *Aonghus*, which
means "unique choice."

Aragorn
For handsome warrior toms,
after the heroic figure in *The Lord
of the Rings*.

Archie
A down-to-earth name for toms.

Ariel
Frin Hebrew, meaning Lion
of God.

Armani
For elegant toms, especially
those with tuxedo markings.

Armstrong
A jazz name for vocal toms, after
famous jazz musician Louis
Armstrong.

Arnie
For muscular, macho cats, after
Arnold Schwarzenegger, famous
for his tough screen persona.

Asterix
For small, brave tomcats, after
the intrepid comic-book Gaul.

Arthur
A noble name for dignified
toms, after the legendary British
King Arthur.

Augustus
An imperial name for
dominating male cats, after
the Roman emperor.

Achilles
A suitable name for warrior
tomcats, after the great hero
Achilles of Greek mythology.

Adolphus
An old-fashioned name for
dignified tomcats.

Adonis
For dazzlingly handsome
tomcats, inspired by Greek

Babbage
For ingenious male cats, after the British inventor Charles Babbage, who conceived the idea of a mechanical computer.

Balzac
A literary name for tomcats, after the nineteenth-century novelist.

Barrington
For imposing tomcats.

Basil
An herb-inspired name for fragrant cats.

Bebop
A jazz-inspired name for cats.

Bentley
A dignified name for tomcats.

Beowulf
For fearless warrior cats, after the hero of Norse mythology.

Bertie
For simple-minded cats, after the P.G. Wodehouse character, Bertie Wooster, whose life is guided by his intelligent valet, Jeeves.

Bilbo
For small, courageous cats, after Tolkien's hobbit hero.

Bogart
A Hollywood-inspired name for rugged tomcats, after the film star Humphrey Bogart, epitome of the tough screen hero.

Boris
An appropriate name for aggressive toms, from the Slavonic *borotj* meaning "to fight."

Botticelli
An artistic name for beautiful male cats, after the Italian Renaissance artist.

Brando
For handsome, tough tomcats, after the rugged film star Marlon Brando.

Braveheart
For warrior toms.

Brubeck
For cool cats, after the American jazz pianist, Dave Brubeck.

Brummell
For elegant tomcats, after the famous eighteenth-century charmer, Beau Brummell.

Brutus
For dominating male cats, after the Roman soldier who joined in the conspiracy to murder Julius Caesar.

Buckingham
A masculine name with regal overtones, after Buckingham Palace.

Buddy
A friendly name for loving tomcats.

Bustopher Jones
A name from T.S. Eliot's *Old Possum's Book of Practical Cats*, given by Eliot to a sleek, black "cat about town."

Buzz
For intrepid tomcats, after the famous astronaut Buzz Aldrin.

Campbell
A Scottish name for male cats, after the ancient Scottish clan.

Cary
A Hollywood name for debonair tomcats, after film star Cary Grant.

Cato
For dignified male cats, after Cato the Elder, the famous Roman statesman.

Cavour
For shrewd tomcats, after the nineteenth-century Italian statesman.

Cayenne
A pepper-inspired name for hot-tempered cats of either sex.

Chairman Meow
For dominating tomcats, after China's leader Chairman Mao.

Chaplin
A Hollywood-derived name for comic tomcats, after silent film star Charlie Chaplin.

Chase
For predatory tomcats who love to chase their prey.

Che
For handsome fighting cats, after freedom fighter Che Guevara.

Chevalier
For distinguished, elegant male cats, after the French singer Maurice Chevalier.

Chinook
A Native American-inspired name for fish-loving cats, after the tribe noted for their salmon-fishing skills.

Churchill
For majestic tomcats, after the British prime minister.

Claudius
For imperial male cats, after the Roman Emperor Claudius I.

Clint
A Hollywood name for long, lean, macho cats, after gun-slinging western star Clint Eastwood.

Clown
For humorous tomcats.

Confucius
For philosophical tomcats, after the famous Chinese philosopher.

Conrad
A literary name for adventurous tomcats, especially those living by the sea; after Joseph Conrad, who set many of his novels in the sea-faring world.

Cornelius
An old-fashioned name for toms.

Cromwell
For tough dominating cats, after the English General, Oliver Cromwell, who overthrew Charles I in the English Civil War.

Cupid
For lovable male cats, after the Roman god of love.

Cyrano
A literary name for dashing tomcats with long snouts, after Cyrano de Bergerac.

Dandy
A dashing name for smart cats.

Dante
A poetic name for thoughtful male cats, after the famous Italian poet Dante Alighieri.

Daredevil
For fearless tomcats who think nothing of taking a risk.

Dean
For rebellious tomcats, after film star James Dean.

Dexter
For mellow toms, after the acclaimed jazz saxophonist Dexter Gordon.

Diablo
For mischievous male cats with a bit of the devil in them, from the Spanish for "devil."

Dickens
A literary name for energetic tomcats, after Victorian novelist Charles Dickens, noted for his prodigious output.

Dizzy
For rhythmic tomcats, after jazz trumpeter Dizzy Gillespie.

Domingo
An operatic name for vocal tomcats, after operatic singer Placido Domingo.

Duke
For cool cats, after jazzman Duke Ellington.

Dylan
For vocal tomcats, after singer and songwriter Bob Dylan.

Earl
An aristocratic name for noble-looking tomcats.

Eiffel
For high-climbing tomcats, after the engineer who constructed the Eiffel Tower in Paris in 1889.

Einstein
For brainy tomcats, after the Nobel Prize-winning physicist Albert Einstein.

Eliot
In tribute to poet T.S. Eliot, creator of *Old Possum's Book of Practical Cats*.

Elton
A pop-inspired name for tomcats, after Elton John.

Elvis
For cats with rhythmic hips; after the king of rock 'n' roll Elvis Presley.

Eros
For lovable male cats, after the Greek god of love.

Errol
A Hollywood-inspired name for dashing tomcats, after film star Errol Flynn.

Excalibur
For brave, sharp-clawed toms, after King Arthur's magical sword, which he pulled out of a stone.

Fonzie
A *Happy Days*-inspired name for charming, cool cats.

Forrest
For cats that like to hunt in the woods.

Fred
A Hollywood-inspired name for agile tomcats, after tap dancer Fred Astaire.

Freud
For thoughtful male cats, after the psychiatrist Sigmund Freud.

Frisco
For laid-back male cats, after the Californian city of San Francisco.

Frodo
For small, intrepid cats, after the hobbit hero of Tolkien's *The Lord of the Rings*.

Gabriel
For angelic male cats, after the Archangel Gabriel, bringer of the Annunciation to Mary.

Galahad
An Arthurian name for noble male cats, inspired by the legends of King Arthur in which Galahad was a shining example of knighthood.

Galápagos
For huge, slow-moving cats, after the Galápagos Islands famous for their giant tortoises.

Galileo
For clever tomcats, after the Italian mathematician, physicist and astronomer.

Gandalf
For wise cats, after Tolkien's wizard in *The Lord of the Rings*.

Garibaldi
For tough, independent-minded male cats; after the Italian soldier who fought for the unification of Italy.

Garrick
For dramatic cats, after David Garrick, the eighteenth-century actor-manager.

Genghis Khan
For ferocious male cats, after the Mongol warlord.

Gershwin
A music-inspired name for elegant tomcats, after composer George Gershwin.

Gillespie
A jazz-inspired name for cool cats, after jazz trumpeter Dizzy Gillespie.

Godfrey
For dignified tomcats.

Godzilla
For destructive, monstrous beasts, after the Japanese monster.

Goldwyn
For dominating male cats, after Hollywood mogul Sam Goldwyn.

Goliath
A biblical name for large toms, after the Philistine giant.

Groucho
For tomcats, after wisecracking Groucho Marx.

Gulliver
A literary name for adventurous male cats, after the hero of Jonathan Swift's satirical novel *Gulliver's Travels*.

Gus
An affectionate monosyllabic name for tomcats.

Haddock
For fish-loving toms.

Hadrian
A Roman name for imperial male cats who like climbing walls, after the Roman emperor who ordered the building of Hadrian's Wall in Britain.

Hagrid
For large but gentle toms, after J.K. Rowling's literary creation.

Hamlet
For thoughtful, noble males, after Shakespeare's Prince of Denmark.

Hammett
A literary name for tough, intelligent tomcats, after the American detective writer, Dashiell Hammett.

Hannibal
For fighting tomcats, after the famous Carthaginian general who took on the Romans.

Harry
For courageous tomcats, after J.K. Rowling's intrepid schoolboy, Harry Potter.

Heathcliff
For handsome, romantic tomcats, after the passionate hero of *Wuthering Heights*.

Hemingway
A rugged name for tough tomcats, after American writer Ernest Hemingway.

Hercules
For strong tomcats.

Hiawatha
For brave tomcats, after the Native American chief immortalized by the poet Longfellow.

Highgate
A London-inspired name for city-loving cats. There is a statue of Dick Whittington's faithful cat on London's Highgate Hill.

Homer
A poetic name for wise tom cats, after the ancient Greek epic poet.

Ivan
A Russian name for imperial tomcats, after Ivan the Great.

Ivor
A music-inspired name for graceful tomcats, after composer Ivor Novello.

Jake
A classic name for tomcats.

Jasper
A stone-inspired name for bright-eyed tomcats.

Jimmy
For cool tomcats, after 1950s heart-throb Jimmy Dean.

Jupiter
A Roman name for kingly tomcats; in Roman mythology, Jupiter was the leader of the gods.

Karloff
A film-inspired name for monstrously large male cats, after actor Boris Karloff, famous for his portrayal of Frankenstein's monster.

Kirk
A *Star Trek*-inspired name for dashing tomcats, after the captain of the Enterprise.

Lancelot
An Arthurian name for handsome male cats, after heroic knight Sir Lancelot.

Legolas
For swift, graceful tomcats, after the elf warrior in Tolkien's *The Lord of the Rings*.

Lincoln
A presidential name for dignified male cats after Abraham Lincoln.

Louis
For regal male cats, after the French Sun King Louis XIV.

Luke
A *Star Wars*-inspired name for adventurous tomcats; after Luke Skywalker.

Machiavelli
For intelligent male cats, after the Italian political theorist Niccolò Machiavelli.

Maestro
For charismatic cats; from the term used for great musical teachers.

Marcel
A Latin name for warring toms.

Marlon
A film-inspired name for tough cats, after film star Marlon Brando.

Marlowe
A tough masculine name for investigative tomcats, after Raymond Chandler's moody private eye Marlowe.

Matisse
An artistic-inspired name for male cats, after the French painter Henri Matisse.

Maturin
For intelligent males, after Stephen Maturin, the doctor hero of Patrick O'Brian's historic naval novels.

Max
A dashing name for suave cats.

Medici
An historic name for dominating male cats, after the Medici family who dominated the Florentine government.

Mephistopheles
A diabolical name for cunning tomcats.

Midshipman
A nautical name for cats.

Mike
A simple down-to-earth name.

Milan
For sleek, urban cats, inspired by the stylish Italian city noted for its fashion scene.

Milton
A poetic name for intelligent tomcats, inspired by the poet John Milton, author of the epic poem *Paradise Lost*.

Mishka
A Russian-inspired name for toms.

Mister
For dignified tomcats.

Mister Incredible
For lovable, portly tomcats, after the animated superhero.

Monet
An artistic name for male cats, inspired by French Impressionist painter Claude Monet.

Monty
For speedy tomcats, after Formula I racing driver Montoya.

Morgan
A swashbuckling name for piratical tomcats, inspired by pirate Captain Morgan.

Mozart
A classical name for male cats, inspired by composer Wolfgang Amadeus Mozart.

Myshkin
A Russian name for dreamy tomcats, inspired by Dostoyevsky's Prince Myshkin.

Natty
For male cats given as gifts, from the Hebrew name Nathaniel, which means "gift of God."

Nemo
For independent male cats, after Jules Verne's Captain Nemo.

Neptune
For regal, water-loving tomcats, after the Roman god of the sea.

Newton
For intelligent tomcats, after scientist Isaac Newton.

Nico
For fighting tomcats, from the Greek *nike* meaning "victory."

Nijinsky
For graceful male cats, after the Russian ballet dancer Vaslav Nijinsky.

Nike
For speedy tomcats, after the popular sport shoe.

Noel
For suave, debonair tomcats, after elegant songwriter Noel Coward.

Odin
For wise tomcats, after the Norse god.

Olympus
For lofty-minded cats, after Mount Olympus in Greece.

Orson
A cinematic name for charismatic, portly tomcats, after actor and director Orson Welles.

Oscar
A Hollywood-inspired name for tomcats with star quality.

Otto
A Germanic name for regal cats.

Palermo
An Italian name for tough cats.

Paris
For chic, city-dwelling cats, after the capital of France.

Parker
For rhythmic tomcats, after jazz saxophonist Charlie Parker.

Percy
For romantic tomcats, after the poet Percy Bysshe Shelley.

Pericles
A Greek name for stately male cats, after the famous Athenian statesman.

Perseus
A mythological name for heroic male cats, after the Greek hero who overcame Medusa.

Pharaoh
An Egyptian name for regal cats.

Picasso
An artistic name for energetic male cats, after Pablo Picasso.

Pollock
For artistic male cats, after abstract painter Jackson Pollock.

Pompey
For combative tomcats, after the Roman general.

Popeye
For tough tomcats, after the muscular sailor man.

Presley
A rock 'n' roll name for charismatic tomcats.

Prince
For noble tomcats.

Puccini
An operatic name for vocal tomcats, after the Italian opera composer.

Pushkin
A literary name for male cats, after Russian poet Alexander Pushkin.

Quentin
An old-fashioned name, especially appropriate for the fifth kitten in a brood, as the name comes from the Latin *quintus* meaning "fifth."

Rajah
For kingly cats, after the term used for Indian rulers.

Rama
For heroic male cats, after the hero of Indian mythology.

Raphael
For beautiful male cats, inspired by the Italian Renaissance painter.

Ray
For cool tomcats, after singer Ray Charles.

Ritz
For elegant tomcats, after the famous London hotel.

Rolex
A jet-set name for sleek tomcats, inspired by the famous status-symbol watch.

Rollo
An old-fashioned name for warrior tomcats.

Rudolf
A balletic name for graceful tomcats that are light on their feet, after Russian ballet dancer Rudolf Nureyev.

Rufus
A dignified name for tomcats.

Runcible
A comic name, derived from the poet Edward Lear's poem "The Owl and the Pussycat."

Ruskin
A literary name for thoughtful male cats, after Victorian art critic John Ruskin.

Sacha
For suave male cats.

Sam
A simple name for tomcats.

Samson
For large, strong cats, after the biblical hero.

Scott
For elegant male cats, after American author F. Scott Fitzgerald.

Scottie
A *Star Trek*-inspired name for earnest male cats, after the engineer on the Starship Enterprise.

Shadrach
A biblical name for courageous tomcats.

Sid
A classic, down-to-earth name.

Siegfried
For brave tomcats, after the legendary German hero.

Slasher
For sharp-clawed killer cats.

Socrates
For philosophical tomcats, after the Athenian philosopher.

Sonny
A musical name for tomcats, after musician Sonny Rollins.

Spartacus
For rugged tomcats, after the gladiator who led a revolt against Rome in 73 B.C.

Spike
For sharp-clawed tomcats.

Spitfire
For fiery-tempered cats.

Spock
A *Star Trek*-inspired name for intelligent, enigmatic tomcats.

Sultan
For regal tomcats.

Teddy
For presidential male cats, inspired by American President Teddy Roosevelt, a great cat-lover.

Tennyson
A literary name for dignified tomcats, after the Victorian poet Alfred Tennyson.

Texas
For large male cats, after the American state.

Thomas
A classic name for tomcats.

Titan
A mythological name for large tomcats, after the giant primeval gods of Greek mythology.

Titus
For strong, rebellious tomcats, after Shakespeare's play *Titus Andronicus*.

Toby
A traditional name, from the Hebrew name Tobias, meaning "God is good."

Toledo
For sharp-clawed tomcats, after the Spanish town famous for its swords.

Tolliver
An old-fashioned name for toms.

Tom
A popular name for tomcats.

Torino
For urban male cats, after the sophisticated Italian city of Turin.

Tristan
An Arthurian name for handsome tomcats, after the dashing knight.

Trombone
A musical name for vocal tomcats.

Trotsky
A Russian name for rebellious male cats, after the Russian revolutionary Leon Trotsky.

Troy
For noble male cats, after the Trojan prince of Greek mythology.

Turpin
A good name for bandit cats, after the notorious highwayman Dick Turpin.

Tuscany
For handsome male cats, after the beautiful, picturesque region of Italy.

Tutankhamen
An Egyptian name for regal tomcats, after the Egyptian boy-king.

Twain
A literary name for lively tomcats, inspired by cat-loving humorist Mark Twain.

Tyson
For tough tomcats, after boxer Mike Tyson.

Valentino
For dashing tomcats, after movie screen idol, Rudolph Valentino.

Verdi
An operatic name for vocal cats, after Italian composer Giuseppe Verdi.

Victor
For fighting toms, from the Latin for "victorious."

Vishnu
For commanding tomcats, after the Vishnu deity.

Vulcan
For fiery-tempered tomcats, after the Roman god of fire.

Waldo
For cats who love the outdoor life, after American essayist Ralph Waldo Emerson.

Walrus
For toothy tomcats, inspired by the male walrus with his large tusks.

Warrior
For fighting tomcats.

Washington
For dignified tomcats, after the first American president.

Wilberforce
An impressive name for tomcats.

William
For regal tomcats, after William the Conqueror, who defeated King Harold at the Battle of Hastings.

Yoda
A *Star Wars*-inspired name for serene tomcats after the diminutive Jedi warrior.

Zachariah
A magnificent, old-fashioned name for impressive felines.

Zeno
For thoughtful tomcats, after the Greek philosopher.

Zeus
For magnificent tomcats, after the Greek god and supreme ruler of Mount Olympus.

Ziegfeld
A showbiz name for flamboyant tomcats, after American theatrical producer Florenz Ziegfeld.

colorful cats

Bianco
For white male cats. From the Italian for "white;" Bianca is the feminine version.

Black Jack
With its licorice associations, an appropriate name for black cats.

Blondie
For golden-haired female felines.

Brandy
A liquor-inspired name for golden-colored cats of either sex.

Bronze
A metal-inspired name for golden-brown-coated cats.

Buttercup
A floral name for golden-furred female cats.

Butterscotch
A confectionery-inspired name for golden-colored cats of either sex.

Apollo
An appropriate name for golden-haired toms, after the Greek god of the sun.

Apricot
A fruit-inspired name for ginger cats of either sex.

Arabica
For coffee-colored cats of either sex, after the high-quality coffee bean.

Bagheera
For handsome black toms, after the noble black panther in Kipling's *The Jungle Book*.

Cappuccino
A chic Italian name for coffee-colored cats of either sex.

Ebony
For attractive black cats, after the highly-prized, dark, tropical wood.

Emerald
A jewel-inspired name for green-eyed cats of either sex.

Felix
An appropriate name for naughty black cats, inspired by the ink-black cartoon cat.

Fudge
For sweet-natured, caramel-colored cats of either sex.

Ginger
A classic name for orange-colored cats of either sex.

Goldie
For golden-furred female felines, after actress Goldie Hawn, with her "dizzy blonde" screen persona.

cat pairs

Bacon and Eggs
Breakfast-inspired names for early-rising felines.

Ben and Jerry
An ice-cream-inspired name for dairy-loving cats.

Bonnie and Clyde
For attractive killer cats, after the notorious criminals.

Castor and Pollux
Heavenly names for inseparable male cats.

Cheese and Crackers
Ideal for hungry cats.

Donner and Blitzen
Teutonic names for a noisy pair.

Fish and Chips
For greedy cats with a taste of fish.

Frasier and Nils
For neurotic egotists, after the popular American TV sitcom.

Gog and Magog
For large, strong male cats, after the giants of folklore.

Jekyll and Hyde
For a pair of schizophrenic cats.

Ketchup and Mustard
For saucy felines after the popular condiments.

Laurel and Hardy
For comic cats, after film comedians Stan Laurel and Oliver Hardy.

Lemon and Lime
Citrus-inspired name for green-eyed cats.

Marx and Engels
Political names for thinking tomcats.

Merry and Pippin
Two hobbit-inspired names for sprightly cats.

Peaches and Cream
For luscious cats.

Raphael and Michelangelo
Artistic names for talented cats.

Rock and Roll
For party cats.

Romeo and Juliet
Shakespearian names for romantic cats.

Romulus and Remus
Roman names for tough tomcats.

Rum and Raisin
An ice-cream-inspired pair of names for sweet cats.

Salt and Pepper
For black and white cats.

Samson and Delilah
For a strong-willed male and female pair.

Sugar and Spice
For sweet-natured cats.

Tom and Jerry
Cartoon names for rush-around felines.

Victoria and Albert
Dignified regal names for a female and male pair.

Yin and Yang
Perfect for philosophic Oriental cats, especially a male and a female.

picture credits

Chris Tubbs Pages 8, 9, 16–17, 19, 25, 26, 27, 30, 31, 35, 36, 38, 39, 40, 42, 45, 56, 57, 59

Andrew Wood Pages 1, 2, 4, 5, 12, 15, 18, 20 both, 21, 22 above, 29 above left & above right, 33, 43, 50, 51, 52, 62

Chris Everard Pages 11, 13, 14, 32, 49, 58

Francesca Yorke Endpapers, pages 53, 54, 55, 60, 61, 64

Polly Wreford Pages 3, 22 below, 23, 46, 47

Jan Baldwin Page 29 below

Christopher Drake Page 6

Tom Leighton Page 7

James Merrell Page 28

author's dedication

For my beloved cats, past and present—
Spiccioli, Mishka, Paris, Sushi, and Felix.

Greymalkin
A traditional British name for gray cats.

Guinevere
For queenly white cats. From the Welsh *gwyn*, meaning "white." Guinevere was the name of King Arthur's beautiful wife.

Guinness
For dark brown and cream toms, after the famous Irish stout.

Harlequin
For acrobatic, patchwork-patterned cats.

Hazel
Nut-inspired name for brown felines.

Henna
For ginger cats of either sex.

Hickory
For smoke-colored cats, inspired by the tree used to flavor smoked meats.

Honey
For golden-brown cats.

Jade
For green-eyed female felines, after the semi-precious stone.

Jaffa
A cookie-inspired name for marmalade-colored cats.

Jamaica
A tropical name for coffee-colored cats, with Jamaica famous for its Blue Mountain coffee.

Jasmine
For dainty white female felines, after the fragrant flower.

Java
A tropical name for coffee-colored cats, after the Indonesian island noted for its coffee.

Jumbo
A suitable name for large, gray tomcats.

Kenya
An African-inspired name for leonine cats of either sex.

Kit-Kat
A chocolate-inspired name for brown cats.

Kiwi
A fruit-inspired name for green-eyed cats.

Lauren
A Hollywood name for beautiful green-eyed female felines, after actress Lauren Bacall.

Lemon
A fruity name for yellow-eyed felines.

Leo
A distinguished name; particularly suitable for tan toms.

Leone
For tawny-tomcats, from the Italian for "lion."

Leopard
For spotted cats of either sex, after the large spotted cat.

Lime
A citrus-inspired name for green-eyed cats of either sex.

Licorice
A candy-inspired name for black cats of either sex.

Lion
For regal, tawny cats, inspired by the "king of the jungle."

Lucille
For comic, ginger-haired female felines, after red-headed comedian Lucille Ball.

Lynx
For cats with large ears and spotted coats, after the wild cat.

Mackerel
A fish-inspired name for striped cats of either sex.

Mandarin
A fruit-inspired name for ginger cats of either sex.

Mango
For sweet-natured ginger cats of either sex, inspired by the tropical fruit.

Marigold
A flower-inspired name for ginger female felines.

Marmaduke
Classic name for marmalade cats.

Marmalade
A domestic name for orange tabbies of either sex.

Marsala
For golden-brown females, after the sweet Italian wine.

Matisse
For colorful cats, after the French artist Henri Matisse, noted for his use of color.

May
A spring-inspired name for white-coated females, after white May blossom.

Midnight
For black cats of either sex.

Milky
For white cats, especially those who like milk.

Mint
An herb-inspired name for green-eyed cats of either sex.

Mist
An atmospheric name for gray cats of either sex.

Mittens
For cats with distinctively colored paws.

Mocha
For coffee-colored cats, after the fine-quality coffee.

Molasses
For dark-furred felines.

Moonlight
For white-furred nocturnal cats of either sex.

Mouse
An endearing name for small gray cats of either sex.

Myrtle
A plant-inspired name for green-eyed female cats.

Nero
For dominating black male cats, after the Roman emperor and from the Italian for "black."

Nutmeg
A spice-inspired name for brown-furred felines of either sex.

Ocelot
For spotted cats, after the Central American wild cat.

Okra
A vegetable-inspired name for slender, green-eyed female cats.

Orange
A citrus-fruit-inspired name for ginger-colored felines of either sex.

Oregano
A culinary name for green-eyed cats of either sex, after the Mediterranean herb.

Orlando
A classic name for marmalade-colored cats, inspired by the hero of Kathleen Hale's illustrated children's books.

Pangur
The name of monk's white cat, immortalized in a famous eighth-century poem.

Panther
For large black cats, after the member of the leopard family.

Papaya
A fruit-inspired name for ginger-furred cats of either sex.

Patch
A down-to-earth name for patchwork cats.

Peanuts
A nut-inspired name for brown-furred cats.

Pearl
A jewel-inspired name for white female cats.

Pecan
A nut-inspired name for brown-furred cats.

Peppermint
A confectionery-inspired name for white cats of either sex, after the mint-flavored candy.

Persimmon
A fruit-inspired name for ginger-colored cats.

Phoenix
For golden-furred, sun-loving cats, after the fabulous golden bird associated with sun worship.

Pierrot
For white tomcats, after the French clown traditionally dressed in white.

Pineapple
A fruit-inspired name for golden, sharp-clawed cats of either sex.

Pistachio
A nut-inspired name for green-eyed cats of either sex.

Puffball
For large, white, fluffy cats, after the giant wild fungus.

Puffin
A bird-inspired name for black and white cats of either sex.

Puma
For large black cats of either sex.

Pumpernickel
For brown-furred cats of either sex, after the German rye bread.

Pumpkin
A vegetable-inspired name for plump, ginger-colored cats of either sex.

Quince
A fruit-inspired name for yellow-furred cats.

Raven
A bird-inspired name for black cats.

Ron
For ginger-haired cats, after Harry Potter's friend, Ron Weasley.

Rosy
A floral name for ginger female felines.

Rum
For golden-brown cats of either sex.

Sage
For gray cats of either sex, inspired by the silver-gray-leafed herb.

Seville
For marmalade-colored cats,
after Spanish Seville oranges
used in making marmalade.

Shadow
For dark gray or tabby cats of
either sex.

Sherry
For tawny cats of either sex, after
the Spanish fortified wine.

Silver
A metal-inspired name for gray
cats of either sex.

Smoky
A classic name for gray cats of
either sex.

Smudge
An appropriate name for cats
with colorful tortoiseshell
markings.

Smut
A homey name for black cats.

Snowball
For white cats of either sex,
especially portly ones.

Snowflake
A pretty name for female
white cats.

Sooty
Perennially popular name for
black cats of either sex.

Sorrel
A plant-inspired name for
reddish-brown cats, after the
plant's red flowers.

Spangle
For spangled cats of either sex.

Spats
A footwear-inspired name for
cats with white or black paws.

Steed
For dapper black tomcats,
after Steed the unflappable
member of the cult TV series
The Avengers.

Stripy
A classic name for striped cats.

Sunflower
A flower-inspired name for
ginger cats of either sex.

Walnut
For brown-furred felines of either sex.

Wellington
For cats with "boots" markings on their paws; after the waterproof boots.

Whiskey
A liquor-inspired name for tawny brown cats of either sex.

White
A self-explanatory name for white cats of either sex.

Yam
A vegetable-inspired name for brown-furred cats of either sex.

Zebra
For striped cats.

Tabby
A classic name for tabby cats of either sex.

Tabitha
A popular name for female tabby cats.

Tangerine
A fruit-inspired name for ginger-furred felines of either sex.

Tansy
An herbal name for ginger-colored felines, after the yellow flower.

Tarragon
An herb-inspired name for green-eyed cats of either sex.

Tawny
For golden-brown cats of either sex.

Tealeaf
A humorous name for brown cats (and/or cats who like to help themselves to treats around your home).

Terracotta
For reddish-brown cats of either sex, from the Italian for "cooked earth."

Tiger
A classic name for stripy cats.

Tigger
The bouncy, exuberant tiger in A.A. Milne's Winnie the Pooh books.

Tiramisu
For coffee-colored cats, after the Italian coffee-flavored dessert.

Titian
An artistic name for ginger-colored male cats, after the Venetian artist noted for his red-headed female models.

Toffee
For caramel-colored cats of either sex.

Topaz
A gem-inspired name for golden-eyed cats of either sex.

Treacle
For sweet-natured black cats of either sex.

Vienna
For cosmopolitan, coffee-colored felines, after the Austrian city noted for its coffee-houses.

Viking
For ferocious ginger-haired toms, after the Scandinavian sea warriors noted for their warlike nature and red hair.

characterful cats

Aquarius
For water-loving cats, after the zodiac sign of the water carrier.

Archimedes
For thoughtful male cats who enjoy sitting in bath tubs; after the Greek mathematician who shouted "Eureka" when he discovered the Archimedes principle while taking a bath.

Artemis
For predatory female cats, after the beautiful Greek goddess of the hunt.

Azure
For blue-eyed cats of either sex.

Bacchus
For fun-loving male cats, after the Greek god of wine and pleasure.

Balthazar
For regal tomcats, after one of the three magi who brought gifts to the baby Jesus.

Bandit
For rogue cats with a flair for thieving.

Beckham
For nimble male cats, after British soccer star David Beckham.

Benny
For loyal but slightly dim toms, after the sidekick in the TV cartoon series *Top Cat*.

Beryl
For green- or blue-eyed cats, as aquamarines and emeralds are both gem varieties of beryl.

Billy
For adventurous tomcats, after outlaw Billy the Kid.

Blondin
For acrobatic male cats, after the tightrope walker Charles Blondin, who walked across a tightrope suspended over Niagara Falls.

Chagall
An artistic name for dreamy male cats, after the Russian artist Marc Chagall, famous for his dreamlike paintings.

Chili
For hot-tempered cats.

Columbus
For adventurous tomcats with an exploring streak, after the famous explorer Christopher Columbus.

Crusoe
For solitary tomcats, after the famous castaway Robinson Crusoe.

Don Juan
For seductive tomcats, after the legendary lover Don Juan.

Dozy
For sleepy cats of either sex.

Epicurus
For male cats, who enjoy good living, after the Greek philosopher Epicurus, who taught that pleasure is the highest good.

Everest
For adventurous high-climbing cats, after Mount Everest, the highest mountain in the world.

Fizz
For lively cats of either sex.

Flitter
For alert, fast-moving cats of either sex.

Fuji
For high-climbing cats of either sex, after Mount Fuji, Japan's highest mountain.

Goth
An historical name for ferocious tomcats, after the Germanic people who invaded the Roman Empire.

Gumbo
A food-inspired name for food-loving tomcats.

Harley
For fast-moving tomcats, after the famous Harley-Davidson motorcycles.

Hector
For fierce tomcats, after the hero of Greek mythology featured in Homer's *Iliad*.

Hercules
For strong, brave tomcats, after the hero of Greek mythology.

Hillary
For tomcats who enjoy climbing and exploring, after mountaineer Sir Edmund Hillary, who reached the summit of Mount Everest in 1953.

Holiday
For vocal female felines, after jazz singer Billie Holiday.

Houdini
For adventurous cats with a penchant for escaping, after the intrepid escapologist Harry Houdini.

Hugo
For dignified male cats, from the Old German Huguberht, meaning "intelligent and noble."

Jack Jack
For strong, saucy kittens after the formidable cartoon baby in *The Incredibles*.

Jaws
The perfect name for killer cats, inspired by Steven Spielberg's 1975 hit film about a ferocious Great White Shark who terrorizes a New England coastal resort.

Joan
For courageous female cats, after fifteenth-century French patriot Joan of Arc.

Kabob
For greedy cats.

Kafka
A literary name for neurotic male cats, after the Czech writer Franz Kafka.

Ladro
For thieving cats, from the Italian for "thief."

Lady Day
For vocal female cats, after jazz singer Billie Holiday, also known as "Lady Day."

Leonardo
For intelligent male cats, inspired by the Renaissance genius Leonardo da Vinci.

Macintosh
For water-loving male cats, inspired by the waterproof coat invented in 1823.

Maple
For sweet-natured cats of either sex fond of climbing trees, after the sugar maple tree from which maple syrup is made.

Marco Polo
For adventurous tomcats, given to exploring, after the famous Italian traveler.

Mercury
For fast-moving cats, after the Roman messenger of the gods.

Merlin
A wizardly name for wise tomcats.

Mick
A rock 'n' roll name for energetic tomcats, after Rolling Stones singer Mick Jagger.

Miles
A jazz name for cool, vocal tomcats, after innovative jazz trumpeter Miles Davis.

Mischief
An apt name for mischievous cats of either sex.

Montezuma
For regal males, after the last Aztec emperor of Mexico.

Mordecai
For water-loving tomcats, after the Babylonian god of water.

Morpheus
For sleep-loving cats, after the god of sleep.

Muddy
A blues-inspired name for mellow tomcats, after blues musician Muddy Waters.

Mustard
A spicy name for hot-tempered felines.

Nantucket
For water-loving cats, after the island off Massachusets.

Napoleon
An imperial name for small but formidable tomcats given to fighting, after Napoleon I, the successful commander who proclaimed himself emperor of France in 1804.

Nashville
For country-music-loving cats, after Nashville, Tennessee.

Nettle
A plant-inspired name for prickly, irritable cats.

Nimrod
For predatory tomcats, after the mighty hunter in the Bible.

Odysseus
A mythological name for intelligent, adventurous tomcats, after the legendary Greek hero of the epic poem *The Odyssey*.

Pavarotti
An operatic name for vocal, portly tomcats, after Italian tenor Luciano Pavarotti.

Pele
For speedy, athletic tomcats, after the great Brazilian soccer player Pele.

Pepper
A spice-inspired name for fiery cats of either sex.

Pepsi
For lively cats, after the popular soft drink.

Pepys
A literary name for nosy male cats, after the diarist Samuel Pepys, noted for his enquiring mind.

Piranha
For felines prone to biting, after the notorious South American fish.

Plato
For philosophical tomcats, after the Greek philospher.

Plum
A literary name for amusing tomcats, inspired by the nickname given to the British humorous writer P.G. Wodehouse.

Porthos
A literary name for greedy and portly tomcats, after the food-loving musketeer from *The Three Musketeers*.

Ra
For lordly male cats, after the ancient Egyptian sun god and lord of creation.

Raffles
A literary name for stealthy male cats, after the famous fictional gentleman cat burglar.

Raleigh
A dashing name for intrepid tomcats given to exploring, after the Elizabethan explorer Sir Walter Raleigh.

Richelieu
For cunning male cats, after the shrewd French cardinal noted for his ruthlessness.

Robin
For adventurous male cats who like climbing trees, after the forest-dwelling outlaw Robin Hood.

Robinson
A literary name for solitary male cats, after the castaway Robinson Crusoe.

Rocky
A film-inspired name for tough tomcats with a taste for fighting, after the boxer played by Sylvester Stallone.

Rousseau
For independent-minded toms, inspired by the eighteenth-century French philosopher Jean-Jacques Rousseau.

Rudyard
A literary name for independent male cats, after the writer Rudyard Kipling who wrote "The Cat That Walked by Himself."

Sagittarius
A zodiac-inspired name for sharp-eyed cats with a flair for hunting; after the sign of the Archer.

Sherlock
For intelligent, inquisitive male cats, after the famous fictional detective Sherlock Holmes.

Shumi
For fast-moving competitive male cats after formidably successful Formula 1 racing driver Michael Schumacher.

Sigmund
For thoughtful male cats, after the famous psychiatrist, Sigmund Freud.

Sinbad
For adventurous, exploring tomcats, after Sinbad the Sailor.

Skipper
A nautical name for commanding tomcats with a taste for water.

Skitter
A pretty name for nervy, fast-moving cats.

Solomon
For regal, thoughtful male cats, inspired by King Solomon.

Sophocles
For dramatic male cats, after the classical Greek playwright.

Sopwith
An aeronautical name for cats with a penchant for heights, after the early plane the Sopwith Camel.

Stella
For night-loving female cats, from the Latin for "star."

Tenzing
For athletic cats with a flair for climbing, after the famous sherpa Tenzing Norgay who reached the summit of Mount Everest in 1953.

Thor
For large, strong, noisy tomcats, after the Norse god of thunder.

Trapeze
A circus-inspired name for acrobatic cats of either sex with a good head for heights.

Ulysses
For clever, adventurous tomcats, after the legendary Greek king also known as Odysseus.

Walter
A literary name for dreamy tomcats, after James Thurber's day-dreaming character Walter Mitty.

Warhol
A pop art name for temperamental tomcats, after artist Andy Warhol.

Winston
For pugnacious tomcats who enjoy fighting, after British Prime Minister Sir Winston Churchill.

Woody
For neurotic tomcats, after film director Woody Allen.

Zorba
For carousing tomcats, after the life-loving literary character Zorba the Greek.

Zorro
For daredevil male cats, after the mysterious black-masked avenger.